THE NEGRO
AROUND THE WORLD

BY

WILLARD PRICE
Author of *Ancient Peoples at New Tasks*, etc.

PICTORIAL MAPS BY
GEORGE ANNAND

ISBN: 978-1-63923-793-7

Printed: March 2023

Published and Distributed By:
Lushena Books
607 Country Club Drive, Unit E
Bensenville, IL 60106
www.lushenabks.com

ISBN: 978-1-63923-793-7

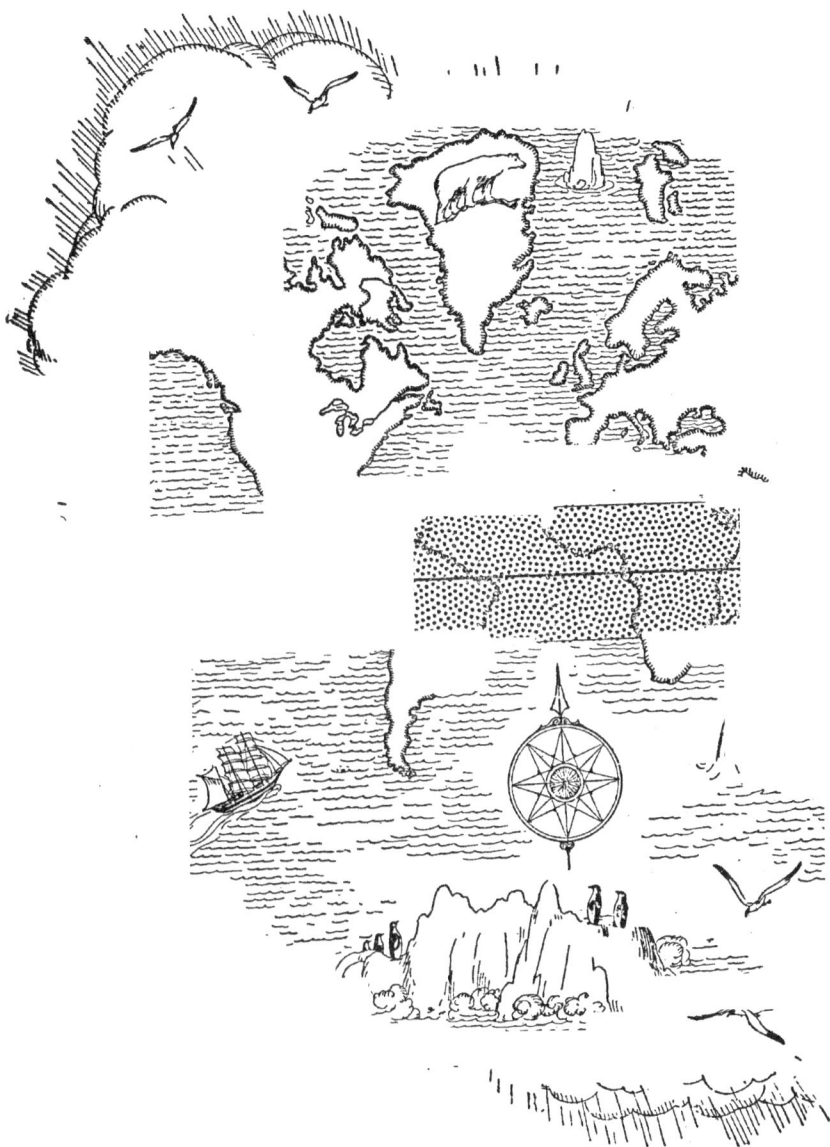

THE BLACK GIRDLE. WITHIN THIS EQUATORIAL
BELT LIVE MOST OF THE 140,000,000 NEGROES OF
THE WORLD.

TO
R. D. P.

CONTENTS

THE NEGRO
AROUND THE WORLD

THE NEGRO AROUND THE WORLD

I

THE BLACK GIRDLE

If an inhabitant of Mars could see the Earth according to the color of its peoples, he could observe a broad black sash about the World's waist.

The belt of black, within which most of the 140,000,000 black people of the globe live, follows the equator and spreads about twenty degrees to the north and the same distance south.

It is not quite broad enough to take in the United States with its 11,000,000 Negroes—but all the other important groupings of blacks in the world are within this tropical belt. It includes the 11,000,000 Negroes of Central and South America and the 10,000,000 of the West Indies. Most of the 100,000,000 Negroes of Africa are found within these limits. The belt continues eastward to take in the scattered millions of the Dravidians of southern India, the jungle dwellers of Indo-China, the pure blacks of the Australasian archipelagoes and the Negritos of the Philippines.

Outside of this black band the black man is an adventurer and a pioneer. Within it he is at home. The blazing equator is his hearth. He is a product of the tropics. The equatorial zone is the nursery and kindergarten of his race. The temperate zone is his university. In the United States, for example, he has graduated to a success he never knew in the tropics. But the tropics have given and still give the greatest impetus to his race in the way of numbers, for there the multiplication is most rapid.

The Martian observer, during the next hundred years, will see the black sash about the Earth's middle grow steadily darker. Black population is now increasing with amazing speed.

Under savage conditions the increase was held in check. Diseases, plagues, slavery, wars between tribes, cannibalism, human sacrifices, ignorance in caring for children, destroyed hundreds of thousands. But as these conditions pass away, population is increasing by leaps and bounds. In the native reservations in South Africa, tribes have increased as much as tenfold in sixty years. It is estimated that, due to the remarkable vitality and fecundity of the race, the black population of Africa will double every fifty years. That means that our grandchildren will see 400,000,000 or more people of the black races in Africa; and an increase of tens of millions elsewhere along the entire length of the black girdle.

It requires no philosopher to see that the effect of these multitudes upon the world of the future depends largely upon the lessons that are being learned in the equatorial kindergarten today.

The scenes of most dramatic development in the future will be Africa and the West Indies; therefore they deserve our chief thought in the pages that follow.

II

GIANT AFRICA

One fifth of the earth's land surface is contained within the continent of Africa.

A traveler who had circled the globe by way of Siberia met one who had circled Africa. They were surprised to find that they had gone the same distance—for it is as far around the coast of Africa as it is around the world.

Africa could easily include all the area of the United States, all China, all India and all Europe, and still have room for twenty Englands in the cracks and corners.

Bigness is characteristic of Africa's life as well as of its territory. It is the home of the elephant, the rhinoceros, the hippopotamus, the giraffe and the ostrich. The richness of the land has given them their enormous proportions. Texas longhorns, transported to South Africa, in a few generations greatly increase in size.

What is the average idea of Africa? A

FRENCH WEST AFRICA

EGYPT

NIGERIA

ABYSSINIA

SIERRA LEONE

LIBERIA

ASHANTI

CONGO

ANGOLA

RHODESIA

PORTUGUESE EAST AFRICA

SOUTH WEST AFRICA

UNION OF SOUTH AFRICA

AFRICA

ONE HUNDRED MILLION NEGROES LIVE IN AFRICA. THERE IS ROOM FOR
HUNDRED MILLION. AFRICA IS ONE-FIFTH OF THE WORLD'S LAND SURFACE
IS AS FAR AROUND THE COAST OF AFRICA AS AROUND THE WORLD.

land of impenetrable jungle and blazing desert, both filled with wild animals.

One humorist says, "I think of Africa as a plain of hot sand bounded on the north by elephants, on the east by lions, on the west by hippopotami and on the south by giraffes."

But there is more to Africa than sand, bush and game for rifle and motion picture camera.

The best alfalfa land in the world is in East Africa. Twelve crops a year can be raised there.

The finest grade cotton comes from Africa. A large share of the world's rubber. More cocoa than from any other continent. Half of the world's gold. Two-thirds of the world's ivory. Ninety-eight per cent of its diamonds.

The coal fields of Africa are as big as four Germanys. Its copper fields equal those of North America and Europe combined. Its iron ore amounts to five times that of North America.

Who lives in this land of enormous wealth? One in every twelve people in the world. White races fringe the edges of the continent, but the center is black. One hundred million Negroes call Africa home. Thus the black population of Africa is nearly equal to the total population, black and white, of the United States.

But there is plenty of elbow room in Africa. There is no crowding—yet.

There are only twelve people to the square mile—as compared with sixteen to the square mile in North America—and 123 to the square mile in Europe!

The additional room will be needed by the most rapidly multiplying race in the world.

Shut away from the world by desert on the north, mountains on the east and jungle on the west, the Central Africans have had little opportunity to know what was going on in other lands. While growing in number, they have almost stood still mentally.

Not only have they been separated from the world. They have been separated from each other. Travel is difficult over marshes and through tangled forests. Tribes a few miles apart do not speak the same language. There are 843 languages and dialects in use among the blacks of Africa. Only a few of the languages have been reduced to writing. Superstition, suspicion, cannibalism and difference of language conspire with the jungle to keep near neighbor tribes apart.

Thus, divided from the world and divided within, the tremendous black power of Africa has been almost powerless.

III

IDLENESS

Imagine that you had been born in Africa. It will help to make graphic just what it means to be a native of the shut-away continent.

Picture yourself dressed in tattoo marks and a necklace of animal teeth—or human teeth, if you happen to be a cannibal. Your hair is oiled and shaped into an elaborate pirouette held in place with a mud plaster.

There you sprawl this sunny morning on the mat in front of your hut. Go to business? Not much! The wife is going to business at the corn-grinder. So you stretch your glistening limbs in the sun, munch your morning croquette of ants, gnats and locusts, and think.

Think—not of the world, because you scarcely know there is one outside of your village; not of what you read in your morning newspaper because you have never seen a newspaper, and the language you speak has never been put into writing; not of business or ambition, of greatness or of God.

No. You think of the flies tickling your toes, of the snake-steak and native beer dinner you had last night, of the evil eye and the witch doctor and of your six children killed by smallpox spirits and lying under the earthen floor of your hut.

Disease-haunted body, cramped thoughts, meager soul, close horizon, low-ceilinged heaven.

With idleness as the corner stone.

Africa is cursed by plenty. Where food may be plucked from the trees or picked up from the ground at will, where the weather is so warm that no clothes are needed and little shelter, why work?

But no race ever yet became great without toil. Idleness would not be so dangerous if it came alone; but it brings after it an endless train of evils. Idleness has sunk the African native in a degradation of mind and body from which he can be lifted only by being taught the attractiveness and value of hard work.

Fortunately, here and there, such teaching

is now going on. Missionaries from American and British churches find they must do more than preach in Africa. There are now many men who, like Alexander Mackay, the first engineering missionary, take as part of their missionary outfit, steam-pipes, cylinders, piston-rods, crank-shafts, pumps and forges, screws and rivets.

Many mission stations, like Lovedale, Mt. Silinda, Old Umtali and the Monrovia College and Industrial Training School (the latter maintained by American Negroes) now teach not only the Bible, reading, writing and mathematics—but agriculture, building, carpentry, engineering and a score of subjects which train character by training the hands.

After natives have carried lumber seventy-five miles out of the jungle on their heads, as in the building of the Monrovia College, they begin to forget the ensnaring joys of idleness.

Africa's industries are growing. There is great demand for workers in all trades. Therein lies hope for the black man of Africa. Torn out of his own idleness, he will yet do something noteworthy for himself and for the world.

IV

WOMAN

An American traveler sat with an African chief. Suddenly a woman rushed up, shrieking and gesticulating. The traveler could not understand her speech. Evidently something very serious had happened. The chief wore a look of tragic horror. But as the woman went on with her story, he suddenly clapped his hands over his mouth and began to laugh. Then he turned to explain the joke to the traveler.

A lion had charged into the garden and carried some one off. At first the chief had thought that a man had been taken. But it turned out to be *only a woman.* It was rather a joke on the husband to lose one of his wives. Outside of this humorous phase of the situation, it meant no more to the chief that a woman had been eaten than if the victim had been a goat.

One man was a bit poorer. He had lost a

bit of living property. Wives are possessions in Africa. They may be, and often are, pawned to pay gambling debts. They are bought and sold. They are cheaper than slaves and easier to manage.

"A man cannot buy or sell slaves now as easily as in other days," says Emily Christmas Kinch, former missionary to West Africa, "so he finds it easier and even cheaper to take a number of wives that they may do the drudgery. As each wife is entrusted with the care and management of a farm or some other of her husband's property, it stands to reason that the more wives a man has, the better his chances of acquiring wealth. Consequently, wealth among the natives is based solely on the number of wives possessed. A man has little or no standing with less than three wives."

At a bargain sale, two inferior wives were sold for one good goat. Sometimes a wife may even be given for nothing—a doubtful gift!

A high class woman among the Tang was sold for the following price: ten goats, five sheep, five guns, twenty wooden chests, one hundred heads of tobacco, ten hats, ten looking glasses, five blankets, five pairs of trousers, two dozen plates, fifty dollars' worth of calico, fifty dollars' worth of rum, one chair and one cat.

A man may sell his own sister to secure money to buy a wife. In certain tribes, when a man dies his son inherits his father's wives and may marry all of them except his own mother.

With the mother of the race ignorantly and cruelly treated, it is no wonder that the race she trains grows up into ignorance and cruelty.

V

SUPERSTITION

She was handsome. Yet she had reached twenty, a late age in Africa, and was still unmarried.

"Why isn't she married?" Mrs. Springer, famous missionary to Africa, asked her house boy.

The boy shrugged his shoulders impressively.

"Why *isn't* she married?" persisted Mrs. Springer. The question had to be repeated several times before the boy reluctantly answered:

"Because she cut her upper teeth first."

Mrs. Springer thought her ears deceived her. But the boy went on to explain.

"In our country it is very, very bad to cut the upper teeth first. A child that cuts the upper teeth first is bewitched and it is the custom of our people to bury such a one alive. I suppose her mother loved her and didn't want to do it, and now there isn't a man in all the country who will marry her."

Of every hundred people in Africa, only three are Christians, thirty-six are Mohammedans—while fifty-eight shrink under the native "religion" which peoples all the air, the woods and every shadow with evil spirits seeking to bewitch and harm man.

While Arab Africa to the north may sometimes find compassion in the heart of Allah, black Africa lives under the dominion of constant fear.

"In their intense fear of ghosts," says Nassau of one tribe, "and their dread of the possible evil influence of the spirits of their own dead relatives, they sometimes adopt a horrible plan for preventing their return. With a very material idea of a spirit, they seek to disable it by beating the corpse until every bone is broken. The mangled mass is hung in a bag at the foot of a tree in the forest. Thus mutilated, the spirit is supposed to be unable to return to the village, to entice into its fellowship of death any of the survivors."

Any man may at any time be accused of witchcraft. That is, the evil spirits have been helping him do harm to his neighbors. He is brought to trial and fed poison. If he dies, and he usually does, he is "guilty."

A chief with 178 wives became ill. Fourteen of his wives were at once clapped into a pen and accused of bewitching their joint spouse. A witch doctor forced each to swallow a hook at the end of a string. The theory was that if they were innocent the hooks could be withdrawn without trouble. But the hooks would not come out, and the fourteen wives were all sentenced to death. Fortunately a missionary arrived in time to save their lives and cure the chief.

Every stick and stone contains a demon plotting against man. Such, in a word, is "religion" in black Africa.

VI

SLOW POISON

In an oasis of the Sahara desert, an Arab invited me to go with him across the blazing sands to the jungles of the black man.

"Why are you going there?" I asked.

"To sell these," he said, pointing to a motley array of pocket mirrors, shoes, razors, colored pictures and a hundred other cheap articles which were about to be bundled up and loaded on the backs of his camels.

"And as I sell," he added, "perhaps I can persuade a few to turn their faces toward Mecca."

The Mohammedan trader is not only a trader—he is a missionary of Mohammedanism. Tens of thousands of Mohammedan missionaries go among the blacks annually, not merely to sell them trinkets, but to cause them to turn their faces toward the "holy city" and repeat the prayer, "There is no God but Allah and Mohammed is his Prophet."

As a result of the work of these trader-missionaries, Mohammedanism is now spreading three times more rapidly in Africa than is Christianity.

The Mohammedan missionary does not demand much. The convert must go through certain prayers and ceremonies. But he is allowed to have as many wives as he pleases; and when he reaches Paradise he will be given seventy-five new and beautiful sweethearts and may also keep the "clay wives" of earth if he wants them.

The fear of evil spirits is removed. So far, so good. But nothing is put in its place. The sins he dared not commit, for fear of demons, he is now free to enjoy.

He is not only free, he is even encouraged in certain vices. Slavery is approved. Lying is praiseworthy if it is skilfully practiced. The great sin of lying is to be caught at it. Mohammed declares:

"A lie is allowable in three cases—to women, to reconcile friends and in war."

As for woman, she "has long hair and small understanding and should rely upon her husband's judgment in all things."

"The evils of European and American civilization," says one traveler, "destroy the black man at once; but the ultimate ideals of that civilization are right and wholesome. There is some hope for those who survive the first onslaughts. But there is little hope for any people that falls under the dead hand of Islam. Mohammedanism injects a kind of slow poison into the very heart of the land."

As taught among the blacks, Mohammedanism is a religion of excused vice, easy morality and supreme laziness. Surely the laziness of the black is enough without adding the indolence of Islam! Of the Mohammedan it has been humorously but quite aptly said that he never runs when he can walk, never walks when he can stand, never stands when he can sit, never sits when he can lie down.

And it is the everlasting lesson of mankind that he who never feels like hurrying physically, will never run very far mentally or morally.

Mohammedanism is chloroform for an already too sleepy continent. It is making a bad situation vastly worse.

VII

AMERICA IN AFRICA

Broadway and Fifth Avenue have gone to Africa.

In one remote African village the sole costume of the chief consisted of a few wildcat tails and a pair of spats. The spats had been manufactured in the garment-workers' district on lower Fifth Avenue.

In another village the natives were crooning an American jazz melody popular on Broadway five years before. Their teacher had been a Pullman porter on the New York Central.

American influence is most evident in Liberia—the republic founded with the help of the United States for former American slaves. The flag is the S T A R and stripes. The capital is Monrovia, named after a President of the United States. The Southern fashions of the days before the Civil War persist, and Liberia displays more frock coats, dress suits and stove-pipe hats in proportion to population than any other country in the world.

Everything from American soap to the American bicycle, has invaded Africa. We now sell Africa more than $50,000,000 worth of merchandise a year.

Ninety per cent of the people of Africa are reached, in one way or another, by our commerce. Not ten per cent are reached by our school teachers and missionaries.

Unlike the Mohammedan trader, the American salesman rarely considers it his duty to enlighten mind and soul as well as to lighten the pocket-book. If he can sell a phonograph today, it does not vitally concern him if his customer is burned for witchcraft or devoured by plague tomorrow.

Missionaries from many American denominations are at work. But they are too few. For every one, there should be a hundred.

"I wish to testify," wrote Richard Harding Davis, "to what seemed to me the enormously important work that is being done by missionaries. . . . In the Congo almost the only people who are working in behalf of the natives are those attached to the missions. . . . It is due to them that Europe and the

United States know the truth about the Congo. They were the first to bear witness, and the hazardous work they still are doing for their fellowmen is honest, practical Christianity."

The extensive work of American Negroes in Africa is little known. Black help to black has been given generously for a quarter century. Anywhere from Sierra Leone to the Cape of Good Hope, in the jungles, on the fertile veldts, near the diamond and gold mines, you are apt to meet a black man bearing on his face the stamp of two hundred years of civilization in America, perhaps a graduate of Harvard or Columbia, who is giving his life to help those of his own color who have not had his opportunity.

He must be a combination of preacher, teacher and doctor—and his wife must be more than that. Industrial schools for boys, institutes to train girls in cooking, sewing, weaving, home-keeping and child care, hundreds of day schools to teach everything from the magic of arithmetic to the use of a toothbrush, churches where spirits of fear are banished by a God of love—these are the gifts of Negro America to Negro Africa.

This is all excellent—yet it is only a beginning. There is but one missionary, white or black, for every 35,000 people. Uncounted millions have never heard one word of modern education or hygiene and know no more comforting religion than that of a demon hiding behind every bush.

VIII

MEDICINE

We arrive at an African village. It looks old, down-at-the-heels. The straw roofs are tumble-down. The whole place shows great age. We expect to see none but old people here—doddering, toothless, white-haired.

Out come the villagers to meet us. They are all young! Not an old man or woman among them. Africa is a land of youth. A continent of boys and girls.

That sounds encouraging—yet the reason is far from encouraging. Africa is a land of young people because the native is picked off by death before he has had a chance to grow old.

The hazards, hatreds and plagues of life in Africa make the man who survives them a miracle.

Epidemics sweep away multitudes. In one district of Uganda, sleeping sickness reduced the population in a year from 22,000 to 8,000.

Entire villages were wiped out by the influenza epidemic in the Belgian Congo, and the number of deaths was estimated as one-eighth of the total native population.

Native medical knowledge is crude. When a man has the toothache he complains:

"The lion in my mouth is roaring."

Some impromptu native dentist will bring an axe, place a wedge of wood against the tooth, give it a blow and dislodge the tooth, perhaps sending it down the patient's throat.

The witch doctor draws heavily upon superstition for his stock in trade. With his needles he will perforate the patient with many holes, in order to let out the evil spirits.

Or through his magic ram's horn he will whisper into his patient's ear, urging the evil spirits to go their way.

Or he will declare that the patient has been bewitched by some one else in the community and insist that that person must be put to death before the sick man can be cured.

In Central Africa one in every two babies dies before he is a year old.

Even in India, only one in five dies. In the United States, one in eleven.

No continent is more sore in body and more

in need of modern medical science than Africa.
The only native doctor is the witch doctor who
kills more often than he cures and is estimated
to be responsible for four million deaths a
year.

There is but one missionary doctor for every
half-million people—while in the United
States there is one doctor for every thousand.

IX

EDUCATION

Writing taps the world's great minds so that all may benefit.

Reading puts a funnel into our mind so that the knowledge of the world may be poured in.

The miracle of "talking paper" has made it possible for the whole world to think and act together.

It is almost impossible for those who accept the ability to read and write as a commonplace, to imagine the isolation of one who lacks that ability. He stands as unaffected by the busy world and its ways as a dead mountain on the cold side of the moon.

There are still many tribes in Africa which know nothing of the magic of written words. Their world is therefore limited to what they can see and hear in their own villages and the nearby jungle.

Only one per cent of the men and one-fourth

of one per cent of the women of Central Africa are literate.

Imagine ninety-nine in every hundred Americans unable to read. Go still farther and imagine that English had never been put into writing—that it remained a spoken language only. Imagine that no English alphabet had ever been invented. Imagine that not a single book, magazine or newspaper existed. There would be no post office—no one could write a letter or read one. There would be no schools worth mentioning, since schools depend mainly upon a written language. The American boy, eager to read, write and learn, would be defeated before he began. Without a written language, civilization would soon crumble. A century or so, and the United States would be broken into several dozen petty nations, each speaking its own tongue; or would become the "protectorate" of some world power able to read and write.

Next to spoken language, written language is the most precious invention of mankind.

Only one African tribe had a written language before the missionaries came.

British and American missionaries set to

work to put the grunts, coughs and hiccoughs of native languages into written words. One aid has been the phonograph, into which a native chief would grunt some well-known story. In five minutes he could make a record which it would take a missionary five months and more to listen to, word by word, and reduce to writing. Many a written language has cost twenty years of a translator's life.

Only a man of the most scholarly intellect and Joblike patience and devotion could possibly accomplish such a task. Yet it is plain that there have been many such men, for 130 African languages have now been reduced to writing!

This means that millions of Africans have at last had the door of world opportunity thrown open for them, thanks to the self-sacrificing toil of missionary scholars; followed by the work of Christian school teachers who, on the basis of reading and writing, are teaching everything from history to soil analysis.

But for millions the door is still locked. More than 700 African languages remain "blind." Their message is for the ear only. It is difficult to find enough men competent to be university presidents in America who are willing to go to the bush of Africa, live in a native kraal and spend the best part of their lives transferring the grunts of an ignorant people to paper.

Yet, without that investment of time and sacrifice, Africa will never make any great contribution to the world.

X

BLACK COLUMBUS

The white Columbus discovered the West Indies in 1492. A shiftless lot of Spanish adventurers followed him. Disliking work, they made the Indians work for them. But the Indians were not strong and died like flies under the brutal treatment of their taskmasters. The Spaniards had now acquired a taste for slavery, and Columbus suggested that Negroes should be brought over.

The black Columbus "discovered" the West Indies in 1502. The first African to be brought to the new world as a slave must have had very different sensations from those of the white discoverer, who had come only ten years before. The black Columbus was not sailing in quest of wealth and fame. He was unwillingly leading the way to the blackest experience of the black race.

Little did he dream of the three and a half dark centuries ahead. Still less did he dream that out of it all would strangely come the most brilliant chapter in the history of his race, which was destined to go farther and accomplish more in six short decades following slavery than in two thousand years of life in Africa.

The indolent African bitterly learned the meaning of toil in the new world. It was the best lesson he could learn, but the method by which it was taught was criminal.

The Spanish masters, and the British and French who soon followed, found it necessary continually to import more slaves to take the place of those who perished under harsh treatment.

More than two million Negro slaves were imported into the West Indies.

When slavery was finally abolished, those who were left began to multiply. At present, there are ten million Negroes in the West Indies.

They live in what would have been one of the richest sections of the globe but for the disastrous cleverness of Napoleon. The sugar cane dripped wealth until Napoleon, his ships driven out of the West Indies by the

The West Indies

The Bahamas

Cuba

Haiti

Virgin Islands

Jamaica

Porto Rico

Ba

South America

British, decided to find a way to ruin the country he could not conquer.

"This day the emperor granted two thousand livres from his private purse to investigate the possibility of making sugar from the beet root," reads the official record.

The successful result of his experiments ruined the West Indies and "the most profitable of islands became the Cinderellas of the nations." The proud sugar cane still waves, but its profits have been cut in two by the humble beet.

The Negroes of the West Indies are now left pretty much to themselves. Ambition has gone elsewhere. The island governments are easy-going and do little either for or against the inhabitants. Laws are loose, schools are few, diseases are many and death comes too early. Several American churches, notably the Protestant Episcopal and the African Methodist Episcopal are doing valuable work. The latter (itself a Negro denomination with 600,000 members in the United States) is carrying on educational and religious missions in Jamaica, the Bahamas, Santo Domingo, Haiti, the Virgin Islands, Barbados and Trinidad.

[49]

The condition of the Negroes in certain of these islands, Haiti for example, is desperate —while in such islands as Barbados they have shown what it would be possible for the race to accomplish everywhere under a system of stern necessity and fair laws.

XI

THE GREEN SERPENT

One cannot visit Haiti and come away without feeling as Roger Babson did that it is "the most backward portion of the western hemisphere." This is Africa on a small scale—a land of barbarism, superstition and ignorance.

Rebelling against their French masters, the Negroes of Haiti threw off the yoke of slavery, established their own republic, and have ruled or misruled themselves ever since. The white was even taken out of the French tricolor. The flag of the black republic has ever since been red and blue.

Having cast out their masters and teachers, as their answer to the brutality of slavery, they have sunk into the other slavery of ignorance. Wander in the interior of the republic of Haiti, or Santo Domingo which occupies the same island, and you will search long to find a man able to read or write. Anyone so giddily intelligent as to be able to add two and two and get four every time is probably possessed of devils.

There is no more weird and ignorant religion in the world than the snake worship or voodoo of the Haitians. The mental, moral and spiritual condition of people who can believe such supernatural trash can hardly be imagined.

A green snake is the god of this religion. A wise snake it is, all-powerful, knowing everything, past, present and to come. If you are a priest ("papa king") or priestess ("mamma queen") of the green snake, you have the power of life and death over your fellows.

Perhaps an official is trying to bring about a reform. He receives warning that his reform is not pleasing to the green snake. If he disregards the warning he may become mysteriously ill or lose his mind. Sacred poisons have been added to his food. Or he may disappear entirely—and in a few months there drifts back from the forest a rumor of slow torture and a cannibal feast.

Needless to say, his brother-officials steer clear of that reform—and of all others that might offend the powers of darkness.

Or a child, who has not even been guilty of

attempting a reform, vanishes. The parents know better than to make any disturbance. The child will never return, and, if they protest, their own lives will be forfeit.

The sacrifice required by voodoo is a "goat without horns" by which is meant a human child, which must be burned alive, its blood drunk and its body devoured. If a child is lacking, a goat or cock may be sacrificed, its blood smeared liberally over the bodies of the worshipers, who indulge in the wildest and most unspeakable debauchery, until morning finds them slumbering in bloody, rum-soaked heaps.

Along the coast, at Port-au-Prince, Santo Domingo City, San Pedro de Macoris, Samana and elsewhere, are a few Christian missions. But they are like a drop of water in a sea of blood.

Slight improvement is also being accomplished by the United States government which has unwillingly assumed loose supervision over the affairs of this blind spot of the western world.

Two and a half million Negroes live in an island amazingly fertile and rich in gold, copper, iron, salt, coal and petroleum. Before

[53]

they can develop it, widespread education will be necessary and a higher moral and spiritual standard than is typified in the worship of a green snake.

XII

NOBODY'S CHILDREN

Man is greater than the animals, partly because of the long period of parental care
enjoyed by human children. Civilization
depends upon this period, to pass on to the
next generation the slowly accumulated experience of the race.

A child without parents is like a nation
without a history. It is an experiment. It
lacks background and foundation. The odds
are long that it will come to grief.

One of the great handicaps of the West
Indies is the presence of hundreds of thousands of illegitimate children, abandoned by
their fathers and often by their mothers as
well, and growing up into a life of dissolute
and ignorant laziness.

According to the last census there are
155,000 illegitimate children in Porto Rico.
"Owing to lack of sufficient orphanages and
children's homes, it is estimated that today

there are 10,000 homeless children on the Island under twelve years of age. The children live on what they can earn, beg or steal. They sleep in the waiting room of a railway station, in the comfortable branches of a tropical tree, or on the porch of some residence. They are entirely illiterate and form the class from which come the beggars and thieves. They constitute a danger to the community, and if it were not for the relatively high death rate that is found among people of this class, the island would soon be overrun by citizens brought up under these criminal-forming conditions."

One-sixth of the men and women of Porto Rico live together without marriage. They are listed by the census as "consentually married," that is, they simply live together by mutual consent, without legal or church ceremony. There is nothing to prevent either or both from walking out at any time and deserting the children. In fact, that is frequently what happens.

The habit of regarding a wedding ceremony as unnecessary is due to the sorry example of the Spanish colonists and the cost of a priest's services, whose charges were so staggering that marriage was put in the luxury class.

Children whom nobody is legally bound to support have always been numerous in Santo Domingo. The American occupation, however, now forces men to pay for the support of their "outside" children. This means that men who have perhaps only three or four legitimate children have suddenly found it necessary to dig up enough money to pay for the food, shelter, clothes and schooling of a young army. Many a pillar of society has twenty-five stray children. One man complained that since he had ninety-two children he could not possibly obey the law requiring him to support them all.

Even more desperate conditions prevail in the Virgin Islands where illegitimacy runs close to eighty per cent. In Jamaica, Cuba and throughout the other islands of "the American Mediterranean" are multitudes of children growing up without rightful parents or homes that they can call their own.

The remedy lies somewhat in strict laws, but more in the education of public opinion against this violation of the rights of children and the future of the West Indies.

XIII

PIRATES

The spirit of piracy still lives in Jamaica.

As we sail into the harbor of Port Antonio we can well understand what an ideal nest this must have been for the pirates of former days. The wind may lash the sea into fury, but this harbor remains snug and calm. Behind it suddenly rise the Blue Mountains in whose deep ravines any amount of loot could be safely hidden.

Just beyond these mountains is the other pirate stronghold, Kingston. Here in the old town of Port Royal, the famous buccaneer, Sir Henry Morgan, the bandit governor of Jamaica, deposited his loot and held wild revels. This town became known as the richest and most wicked spot in the new world.

Then one day, as if in judgment, an earthquake sank most of Port Royal beneath the sea. On safer ground a new capital was built and called Kingston. Today the ships

[58]

sailing into Kingston harbor pass over the very spot where the tipsy revels of the buccaneers were once held. On stormy nights, say the superstitious, you may still hear the tolling of the cathedral bells of Port Royal, fathoms deep beneath the waves.

Landing at Kingston, you are led to believe that the present inhabitants are doing their best to imitate the buccaneer fathers of their country. A more insolent and mischievous crew it would be hard to imagine. No girl, white or black, is safe on the streets of the capital after dark. Even a man will do well to remain indoors unless he is one of a sufficient number to do battle with a gang of hoodlums, if need be.

Assaults and robbery are common even in broad daylight. Things disappear as if by magic. A respectable, old Negro poet, whose most precious possession was a new set of false teeth, dropped off to sleep while sitting on a park bench; when he awoke his teeth were gone! Anything, as small as a pin or as large as a house, may be stolen. Food melts. Vegetables vanish from the garden before they are ripe. Plump chickens live constantly in the shadow of death. Cows come home at night with empty bags—or do not come home at all. The farmer gazes upon his ripe crop in the light of the setting sun; at sunrise he goes out to harvest it and finds that someone has saved him the trouble.

Prosecutions for the stealing of growing crops nearly doubled in the year following the war. The "teefing" of small articles is amazingly common. Jails dot the island and are much more in evidence than schools.

It is easier to "teef" than to work. Jamaica accommodates 868,000 Negroes and 17,000 whites and the island is large and bounteous. The weather is gentle and there is no grim necessity. Work is "too much boderation." The Sabbath is apt to begin Friday night and continue until Tuesday morning—with a "hangover" for the rest of the week.

Although Jamaica has been a possession of the British crown longer than any other land except Barbados, little has been done to educate, train and develop the Negro population. Thanks to his basic racial qualities of cheerfulness, idealism and mental alertness, the present black pirate of Jamaica could, under proper training, be turned into a valuable citizen.

XIV

A TIGHT LITTLE ISLAND

The population of Barbados is more dense than that of any other land in the world, except China.

There are 1,200 people to the square mile. You may easily walk the length of the island in a day—yet it contains 200,000 people, 180,000 of whom are black.

Squeezed into this geographical corset, the population of Barbados is nevertheless as good natured and industrious a group of people as one could find anywhere on the globe. In striking contrast with the indolent pirates of Jamaica, the residents of Barbados are constantly and courteously on the job. The Jamaican Negro illustrates the sorry result of man's neglect and nature's bounty. The Barbadian is evidence of the wholesome effect upon Negro character of a keen, clean struggle for existence.

Hard work is the great tuner of men's souls.

And hard work is necessary where 1,200 people must wring a livelihood out of the agriculture or trade that can be conducted on one square mile.

In a climate of perpetual June, sugar and cotton are vigorously and successfully cultivated. But not all can be farmers in such a pocket-handkerchief of an island, and the man who is not a farmer in Barbados is apt to be a shop-keeper. Even the shanties along the wayside bear shop signs, and anything from a cracker to a suit of clothes may be purchased within.

"The Yankees of the West Indies" the Negroes of Barbados have been called and certainly they are so energetic that the Jews cannot stand the competition. Not only the Jews, but the Portuguese, Chinese and Syrians, born tradesmen all, give Barbados a wide berth. In other islands they reap a harvest, but they cannot keep up with the black merchants of Barbados.

Even the undertakers go after trade with brisk enterprise. Some of their advertisements are a trifle peculiar, but evidently they get the business. "Why trouble yourself over the dead," queries one advertisement, "when you can see the up-to-date and experienced undertaker face to face? Look for the hearse with the GOLDEN ANGEL." Not content with prose, the advertising undertaker then breaks into poetry. He requires twenty-four verses to tell all the advantages one may enjoy in being buried by him.

Since the British rule both lazy Jamaica and busy Barbados, it is obviously difficult to pin upon the rulers the blame in one case or the credit in the other. Evidently the difference is in the islands themselves. In bountiful Jamaica, Nature pampers man, as if he were an only child. But in pinched Barbados, Nature has so many children that each must shift for himself.

Courtesy is compulsory in Barbados. People so crowded must learn to get along with each other. After the rowdyism encountered elsewhere, the politeness, sweetness and busy good nature of the Barbadian are charming. There can be no doubt that many of the virtues of the Barbadian are due to the consistent Christian campaign that has been carried on in the island. His religion is far removed from the savage devil-dread of Africa.

Although still lacking adequate church and school provision, he is a vivid example of the ability of his race to sweeten and ripen under the stimulus of a hard job and a fair chance.

XV

HOLLAND IN CHARCOAL

We sail on toward South America—but, before reaching it, we pass that racial rainbow, Trinidad.

Probably there is no race under the sun that is not represented in the Island of Trinidad. Yellow, red, white, black, grey, chocolate and "India tint"—from China, Egypt, India, Venezuela, Sweden and other lands the world over—they have voyaged to this island melting pot and have "suffered a sea change into something rich and strange."

In Port of Spain, Penal, St. Joseph and elsewhere there are large Negro communities, but they too have been strongly influenced by the world current flowing around and through them. Trinidad has been called "the world in miniature." It is truly a racial cross-section of mankind.

This is the last of the stepping-stones to South America—and we now set foot upon the continent itself. We find ourselves in a sort of black Holland. Both British and Dutch Guiana are Dutch in character. The first, although now under British rule, was originally settled by the Dutch, and the influence of its early owners is still much in evidence. Dutch Guiana, on the other hand, was first occupied by the British, who gave it to the Dutch in exchange for the "New Netherlands," now known as New York.

What a trade! The "New Netherlands" now has a population of nearly eight millions; Dutch Guiana has few more than a hundred thousand people. The "New Netherlands" contains the second city, or shall we say the first, in the world; Paramaribo, the capital of Dutch Guiana is one-half of one per cent the size of New York.

Yet, for quaintness and charm, New York stumbles far behind Paramaribo, this lovely bit of Holland stuck like a tulip in the lapel of South America. Here are the canals of old Holland, the steeply-arched Dutch bridges, tiny-paned windows, brick stoops, projecting dormers and gables like old-fashioned bonnets, flowers everywhere attracting the butterflies and humming birds.

And the people—they are Dutch too, but with a difference. From the rear they look Dutch enough. That woman with a turban pointed like a Dutch cap, with a short stiff cape of bright calico, with flaring skirts puffed with petticoats and tucked into huge rolls about the waist, yes, even wooden shoes—surely she is all Dutch and nothing but.

' She turns—her face is black! She speaks— and instead of the Negro "Yas sah" of the British West Indies she says "Yah, mynheer," and rumbles along in the guttural language of the land of windmills. She reads the Dutch signs over the shop doors. She buys Dutch cheeses and she pays for them in guilders. Almost three hundred years of Dutch rule have made her race quite Dutch, except in skin.

The Dutch Negroes of the Guianas are on intimate terms with soap and water. They have acquired the Dutch reverence for cleanliness as akin to Godliness, nor have they any mean respect for the latter. They have a keen desire for education, but schools are few. Missionary schools such as the Fountain Collegiate and Industrial Institute in Georgetown not only teach the three R's but give much needed training in industries, sewing, needle work and home making.

Black Holland, like the pink-and-white Holland of the north, is thrifty. Her people work hard, and in the main, soberly. British and Dutch Guiana combined, export more than they import, which means that they are not merely dependent upon the rest of the world, but contribute something to it. That something consists of sugar, rice, coconuts, coffee, rubber, gold and diamonds; indicating a country rich in resources; while richer still in the character and possibilities of her people.

XVI

AFRICA IN AMERICA

One of the greatest racial miracles of all time has occurred in America. The black race, brought to the New World as involuntary "pilgrim fathers" under the yoke of slavery, has turned the tables upon Fortune by rising to a higher stage of development here than anywhere else in the world.

In his first thirty years after release from slavery, the American Negro, declares Lord Bryce, made greater advance than was ever made by the Anglo-Saxon in a similar period.

Not only in North America, but in Central and South America which together contain more than 11,000,000 Negroes (9,000,000 in Brazil alone) the race has gone swiftly forward. The most startling progress, however, has been made among the 11,000,000 Negroes of the United States.

In education, even Lord Bryce's Anglo-Saxon has never experienced such pell-mell

advance. When freedom was declared, not
3 per cent of the Negro race in America could
read or write. Now 80 per cent are literate.
Mr. Henry Watterson, prominent Kentuckian,
who used to own slaves, has said,

"This indicates a progress in education
which is greater than any other race in history has ever made."

Stimulated by constant contact with a
vigorous white population in a new and
rich land, and possessing the innate ability
to go forward, the Negro in the United States
has made these advances in just over fifty
years:

Homes owned by Negroes have increased
from 12,000 to 650,000.

Farms operated by Negroes have multi-
plied from 20,000 to 1,000,000.

Businesses conducted by Negroes—from
2,100 to 60,000.

There were 600 Negro teachers—now
43,000.

Voluntary contributions by Negroes to education have grown from $80,000 a year to
$2,700,000.

Negro churches—from 700 to 45,000.

Sunday school pupils—from 50,000 to 2,250,000.

And church property has increased sixfold, from $1,500,000 to $90,000,000.

The American Negro's land holdings now amount to more than 20,000,000 acres, an area equal to New England if Maine is omitted.

There are now more than one thousand patents issued for inventions by Negroes.

Formerly the black depended upon the white for everything. Now he depends upon his own race. He has his own Negro lawyers, judges, surgeons, nurses, dentists, authors, actors, architects, chemists, his own banks and newspapers.

Yet, while he has developed a life of his own, he has entered into the life of his country—in so far as he is permitted to do so.

Two million dollars were subscribed by Negro patriots to the United War Work Drive. Four hundred thousand Negroes took part in the World War. How did they fight? To list their decorations and citations would fill a book. But it is all summed up in the remark of a French officer who gave his seat to a Negro woman in a crowded New York subway train,

"It is an honor," he said to a bystander, "to give my seat to an American Negro. I saw the Negro troops fight in France!"

In citizenship, morality, knowledge and industry, the American Negro, in spite of discrimination and lack of proper educational opportunity, compares favorably with the general American average. Such a meteoric rise from savagery to civilization in a few short generations is sensational proof that any labor the world may choose to spend in training the black race as a whole will not be labor lost.

XVII

FUTURE

There are two chief factors in the future of the black race.

One is its amazingly rapid increase in numbers.

The other is the equally amazing rapidity with which it progresses wherever it is brought under progressive influences.

If the swift multiplication of blacks can be kept under a steady stream of right influences, the race will grow in character as it grows in numbers.

This is easiest in America, more difficult in the West Indies, most difficult in Africa. In America there are many civilizing forces. In the West Indies and particularly in Africa, civilization stumbles far behind in the race with ignorance, superstition and disease.

The world has long since learned that suffering or backwardness in one land is sure to be reflected in other lands. The handicaps of one race handicap the whole human race, just as certainly as the poor playing of one member of a football team reduces the score of the whole team. Therefore the problem of Africa and the West Indies is the world's problem.

Governments in the lands concerned might increase tenfold their educational and socializing efforts without in the least overstraining themselves. British and American missionary organizations are doing valuable work, although one of the greatest American denominations is not represented in the entire continent of Africa with the exception of the tiny republic of Liberia.

Although the problem should concern everyone, of every land and color, it should appeal most strongly to the Negro himself. Why should not the Negro of the United States, who has been swept into a success unknown to his people elsewhere, take chief responsibility for the welfare of his race in other lands?

There is one Negro in the United States for every ten in Africa. The one is many times richer than all ten put together, knows more, and does more real work in one day than the ten in ten days. Thanks to his own advancement he is in a position to give knowledge for ignorance, health for disease, religion for superstition.

Perhaps he cannot go personally to the jungle or the veldt—but through racial organizations and particularly through the missionary societies of his own churches organized for this special purpose, he can extend his own swiftly won advantages to others who are less fortunate.

He can ride his dollar across the sea and make his influence felt in at least ten lives somewhere within the "black girdle."

Without some such united effort as this, the equatorial zone, while multiplying in numbers, will multiply also in ignorance, superstition and plague. That, the world can ill afford. It is in violation of all rules of efficiency—not to mention those of humanity.

www.ingramcontent.com/pod-product-compliance
Lightning Source LLC
Chambersburg PA
CBHW051504270326
41933CB00021BA/3462